# GOING BEYOND ABRAHAM'S BLESSING

FREDERICK TAYVIAH

**Trafford**
PUBLISHING

Order this book online at www.trafford.com/07-0944
or email orders@trafford.com

Most Trafford titles are also available at major online book retailers.

© Copyright 2007 Frederick Tayviah

All rights reserved. No part of this publication may be reproduced, stored in a retrieval system, or transmitted, in any form or by any means, electronic, mechanical, photocopying, recording, or otherwise, without the written prior permission of the author.

Note for Librarians: A cataloguing record for this book is available from Library and Archives Canada at www.collectionscanada.ca/amicus/index-e.html

Printed in Victoria, BC, Canada.

ISBN: 978-1-4251-2749-7

*We at Trafford believe that it is the responsibility of us all, as both individuals and corporations, to make choices that are environmentally and socially sound. You, in turn, are supporting this responsible conduct each time you purchase a Trafford book, or make use of our publishing services. To find out how you are helping, please visit www.trafford.com/responsiblepublishing.html*

*Our mission is to efficiently provide the world's finest, most comprehensive book publishing service, enabling every author to experience success. To find out how to publish your book, your way, and have it available worldwide, visit us online at www.trafford.com/10510*

**Trafford** PUBLISHING   www.trafford.com

**North America & international**
toll-free: 1 888 232 4444 (USA & Canada)
phone: 250 383 6864 ♦ fax: 250 383 6804 ♦ email: info@trafford.com

**The United Kingdom & Europe**
phone: +44 (0)1865 722 113 ♦ local rate: 0845 230 9601
facsimile: +44 (0)1865 722 868 ♦ email: info.uk@trafford.com

10 9 8 7 6 5 4 3 2

# Dedication

This book is dedicated to God the Father, the Son, and the Holy Spirit for giving me the honor and entrusting me with a deep understanding of His truth, His love, and the power of His covenant with man through Christ Jesus. I thank the Lord that He gave me the ability to put this into writing.

I also thank the following for their support and help with the completion of this book.

My dear wife Arlette, a woman of God who took extra time with our two children, Elikem and Mawutor-Angelle, when ever I needed peace and quiet to write this book.

My mother-in-law Milcah Huggins, a God fearing woman who made me cups of tea when I stayed up late at nights after work to write.

My sister-in-law Hera Huggins, a woman of God,

a graphic designer, who came up with designed cover of this book within days after I told her the title of this book.

My sister-in-Christ Linda Gillespie, a woman of God who happily accepted, read through this book and edited it.

I can not thank any of you enough, so I pray that God reward you all greatly.

# CONTENTS

Chapter 1 - Going beyond Abraham's blessing
Chapter 2 - The Holy Spirit
Chapter 3 - Ability to hear from God
Prayer of Salvation
Scripture verses are from The New International Version

# CHAPTER 1

# GOING BEYOND ABRAHAM'S BLESSING

*But you, Israel, are my servant, Jacob whom I have chosen. The descendants of Abraham my friend. (Isaiah 41:8)*

God called our father of faith Abraham, His friend. We have read in the scriptures how Abraham obeyed God, had a covenant with God and was blessed in every way.

In the book of Galatians 3:14 it is written:

*He* (Christ Jesus) *redeemed us in order that the blessing given to Abraham might come to the Gentiles (Christians) through Christ Jesus, so that by faith we might receive the promise of the Spirit.*

The above scripture verse is a true statement. It was Abraham's faith in God, his obedience to God's words that brought about those wonderful blessings of God that we have heard so much about. We who believe and have faith in our Lord Jesus Christ today are also blessed with the blessing of Abraham, the man of faith.

The scripture tells us,*"The just or the righteous will live by faith."*

It is a good thing to desire Abraham's blessing, not only the material side of his blessing but also the spiritual side.

Whenever we (Christians) hear of Abraham's blessing, the first thing that comes to mind is the material blessing. We forget that he had to seek God first, and he was able to hear clearly from God. Without questioning God, Abraham did whatever he was told or what was requested of him. That means he had a wonderful, intimate relationship with his Creator, the Almighty God. Abraham was favored by God, and everything that came to him was blessed. God further honored Abraham by calling him His friend. The scripture tells us, *"Abraham believed the Lord and He credited it to him (Abraham) as righteousness."*

## LOOK BEYOND THE MATERIAL BLESSING

As people **redeemed by our Lord Jesus Christ**,

we have to look beyond Abraham's material and physical blessings. We should pay special attention to the spiritual blessings of our Lord Jesus Christ, our Redeemer, available to us when we received Him as Lord of our lives.

I was meditating on Jesus Christ our redeemer and educating my soul on the words, ***"in Christ Jesus"***. During that time much was revealed to me. Now I would love to share with you, all that was revealed to me by His Spirit.

The statement, ***"In Christ Jesus or in Him"*** has appeared in the scriptures of the New Testament so many times. There is a reason why God has allowed it to be written a number of times. It is for our remembrance and our own good, to know that there is power in Christ Jesus alone. God the Father wants all who are redeemed and name the name of our Lord Jesus Christ to know that we are not independent of our Lord Jesus, but fully dependant on Him (the Lord). The only way we believers can make it through this dark world is to let go of ourselves and allow our lives to be plugged <u>in Christ Jesus</u> and take root in Him.

When we are in Christ Jesus, nothing can move us. If there is anything in this world that He has created that can ever move Him, then that thing can also move us, but I know not one. He is the Creator, the unmovable One.

To be in Christ Jesus is not just words of our mouths, but our heart (spirit) soul and body should be in it. We have to train our soul and body to respond to the statement <u>in Christ Jesus</u>. So many times we say we are in Christ, but our heart is really not in what we say. Then what we say becomes only word of mouth, without power, because we do not say it with heart conviction, or it is not said in faith. We have to go beyond just words of the mouth, and train out heart (spirit) and (soul) mind daily to say words of faith with conviction. That is the only way we can be grounded in our faith in Christ Jesus. Until we become one in spirit, soul and body, with what we say, it will be difficult to experience the wonders of the Lord that the scripture talks about.

It is in Christ Jesus that we have our being. Our strength comes from the Lord.

Let us talk a little about our father of faith, Abraham. Abraham was called by God. It was because of his obedience to do whatever God instructed him that he found favor with his Creator. It was because of his belief in God that he won the heart of God and was blessed materially. It was through Abraham's faith in God that God found it necessary to make covenant with him. This covenant was a covenant of love, favor, obedience and blessings. It is a covenant of love because there were millions of people in the world at that time, but God chose to call him alone. It was not because Abraham was more righteous than all the people on earth but because of God's favor upon his life.

God, knowing Abraham's heart, knew he had a heart to love Him (God) and a heart willing to obey his God. God said in His word, *"If you are willing and obedient, you will eat the best from the land."*

Yes, Abraham was more than willing and obedient to God. For that reason, God honored His word, opened the windows of heaven, and poured out His blessings on Abraham. His blessings were the best of the land and good health.

## THE OLD AND THE NEW COVENANT

We know and understand the truth that all those who believe in the Lord Jesus Christ today are also children of Abraham. God justifies all who believe in Christ Jesus by faith. Now, we who believe in Christ Jesus have a higher and better covenant. Someone may wonder why our covenant in Christ Jesus is better than the old covenant. To answer that, let us take a good look at both of them and it will be plain which one is the final and a better one.

## BLOOD COVENANT

In Genesis 15:9-21 God said to him (Abraham):

9. *"Bring me a heifer, a goat and a ram, each three years old, along with a dove a young pigeon.*
10. ***Abram*** *(*a name before it was changed by God to Abraham*) brought all these to Him, cut them in two and arranged the halves opposite each other, the birds however, he did not cut in half.*
11. *The birds of prey came down on the carcasses, but Abram drove them away.*

12. *As the sun was setting, Abram fell into a deep sleep, and a thick and dreadful blackness came over him.*
13. *Then the Lord said to him, Know for certain that your descendants will be strangers in a country not their own, and they will be enslaved and mistreated four hundred years.*
14. *But I (the Lord) will punish the nation they serve as slaves, and afterward they will come out with great possessions.*
15. *You, however will go to your fathers in peace and be buried at a good old age.*
16. *In the fourth generation your descendants will come back here, for the sin of the Amorites has not yet reached its full measure.*
17. *When the sun had set and darkness had fallen, a smoking firepot with a blazing torch appeared and passed between the pieces.*
18. *On that day the Lord made a covenant with Abram and said, "To your descendants I give this land from the river of Egypt to the great river, the Euphrates.*
19. *The land of the Kenites, Kenizzites, Kadmonites.*
20. *Hittites, Perizzites, Rephaites.*
21. *Amorites, Canaanites Glrgashites and Jebusites.*

Every word that God spoke to Abraham was sealed with the blood as covenant. All that God spoke into Abraham's life came to pass. The promises which were to be fulfilled in his life time all came to pass; and the rest were fulfilled after his death as God had indicated would happen. In all, it was a wonderful covenant, but the reality is that Abraham's covenant was a shadow or a copy of the real one to come through Jesus the Christ.

Some one may ask; did not Moses and the people of Israel have yet another covenant with God? The answer is that they did not have a new covenant apart from Abraham's covenant. For if we read carefully, verses 13-14 and 16 of the above scriptures, we can see they were included in the covenant that God made with Abraham. God told Abraham to know for certain that his descendants will be strangers, enslaved and mistreated in a country not their own, for four hundred years. After that they would come out with great possessions. Those descendants were the people of Israel that Moses led out of Egypt. Were they slaves in a country that was not their own? The answer is yes! Were they there in Egypt the years that Lord had indicated? The answer is yes! And they came out with great possessions, as the Lord had told Abraham they would.

As they were already included in the first covenant and they came to the land God had already promised Abraham their forefather, what God did with Moses and the people of Israel was a renewal or restoration into the covenant made with Abraham, when they got out of Egypt and entered into the promised land. The descendants of Abraham continued with animal sacrifices just as he (Abraham) had done.

In addition they had the ten commandments of the Lord and other laws, which were sealed in the blood of animals. Their ceremonial sacrifices went farther as God instructed them to offer animals for their sins. In Hebrews 10:3-7, we read:

*3. But those sacrifices are an annual reminder of sins.*
*4. Because it is impossible for the blood of bulls and goats to take away sins.*
*5. – 6. Therefore, when Christ came into the world, He said: "Sacrifice and offering You did not desire, but a body You prepared for Me; with burnt offerings and sin offerings You were not pleased.*
*7. Then I said, "Here I am it is written about Me in the scroll I have come to do Your will O God."*

In the Law of Moses, the law required that these sacrifices and offerings be made. But when Jesus came, scripture tell us that God Almighty does not desire those animal sacrifices but had prepared Him (Jesus) to be offered. Jesus was very willing to do the will of the Father to the end. He gave His own Body as a living sacrifice onto the Lord, and in His own blood He set aside the first covenant to establish the second, which we call the New Covenant.

Truly, the real and final covenant that does not need the blood of goats or other animal sacrifice exists right now in the New Covenant in Christ Jesus and is sealed in Jesus' own precious BLOOD. We have been made holy through the sacrifice of the body of Jesus Christ once and for all.

## COMPARING THE OLD AND THE NEW

Let us look again at Abraham's covenant. God called him out of his country, away from his people and his father's household, to a land that God showed to him (Genesis 12).
Why did God do that?
It is because God wanted to separate Abraham from his people, for they could have influenced his faith. God set him apart and used him for His own glory. In the same way, in the new covenant through Christ Jesus, we (who are saved) have been called from the darkness of this world into the light of God. We were taken from the dominion of sin into the righteousness of God through Christ Jesus. We have been set apart, separated for the Lord's use.

In the old covenant, God promised Abraham a son and descendants who would be enslaved. Then, after a set time, He (God) would bring them out to take over the Promised Land. This promise of God to Abraham was sealed with blood of animals. And all came to pass as we already know. In the new covenant, God the Father promised the world His only begotten Son, Who would take our infirmities and carry our sorrows, He was to be pierced for our transgressions, and would be crushed for our iniquities. His punishment was to bring us peace and by His wounds we are to receive our healing. He was to unite all mankind who would believe in Him, with God the Father.

All these promises were fulfilled; God gave His only Son (Jesus Christ), who fulfilled them all. Instead of animal sacrifice, our Lord Jesus Christ went on the cross and shed His precious blood as atonement for our sins. His precious blood has Life and Power since the day it was poured on the cross up to this day; and it will always be the same till the end of the world.

We read from Genesis 15, that God asked for a heifer, a goat, a ram, and each had to be three years old. When the animals were sacrificed by Abraham the Bible tells us he kept watch, then fell into a deep sleep and a thick and dreadful darkness came over him and the Lord spoke with him. After that, when the sun had set and it was dark, a smoking firepot with a blazing torch appeared and passed between the pieces of the sacrificed animal. On that day a covenant was made with Abraham.

In the new covenant in which Jesus Christ was the sacrificial lamb, Jesus began His earthly ministry and was crucified within three years. As a sacrificial lamb, He was three years old in His mission to do the will of God on earth. In Abraham's covenant, God demanding the sacrifice of three year old animals shows that covenant to be the shadow or a copy, of the real and final sacrifice of the Lamb of God, Jesus Christ, on the cross.

When Abraham made his sacrifice he fell asleep and experienced a dreadful darkness.

In the new covenant, when Jesus Christ was crucified, it is reported in Mark 15:25, 33-34, that:

*25."It was the third hour when they crucified Him.*
*33.At the six hour darkness came over the whole land until the ninth hour.*
*34.And at the ninth hour Jesus cried out in a loud voice, "Eloi, Eloi, lama sabachthani" which means, My God, My God why have You forsaken Me?"*

When the Lamb of God (Jesus Christ) was sacrificed and the sins of the world were laid on His back, at the sixth hour from the time He was nailed on the cross, a complete darkness came over the land. It lasted for three hours. What was shown in the shadow (the old covenant), was repeated in the real (the new covenant), revealing that it was the sins of the world that came over the Lamb as darkness. He bore our sins in His own body. Through Him we are forgiven of our sins.

The reason Abraham cut the sacrificed animals into two and walked between them, and the smoking firepot with a blazing torch passed between the pieces, was that God was showing what would happen in the new covenant. When the Lamb of God (Jesus Christ) breathed His last breath, it was reported in the book of Mark 15:38, *"The curtain of the temple was torn in two from top to bottom"*.

This curtain of the temple that was reported torn

in the above scripture came about when God instructed Moses to make a tabernacle of His presence, which Moses built for the Lord. The tabernacle was in three sections: the outer court, the inner court, and the Holy of Holies. Because of the sins of the people, God instructed Moses to make a curtain separating the inner court from Holy of Holies. It meant, in those days before the new covenant in Christ Jesus, that the sins of the world were like a curtain, separating man from God.

When Jesus bore the sins of the world in His body and paid the ransom for man with His own blood, God the Father forgave man of their sins. God the Father demonstrated His acceptance of Jesus' sacrificial death on the cross for our sins by tearing from top to bottom, the curtain in the temple. This wonder of God shows that there is no longer separation between man and God.

In the same way God allowed Abraham to walk freely between the sacrifice, and the blazing torch passed between the pieces, in the new covenant through Jesus Christ, we who believe can come freely before the throne of grace without facing the wrath of God. This is because we are justified by the blood of the Lamb, and all who believe in Him are sealed in Christ with the fire of the Holy Spirit. The Holy Spirit is a deposit guaranteeing our inheritance until the redemption of those who are God's possession, to the praise of His glory.

## SEEKING GOD FIRST

*"But seek ye first the kingdom of God and His righteousness, and all these things shall be added unto you." (Matthew 6:33).*

As mentioned previously, the first thing we associate with Abraham's blessing, whenever we hear it mentioned, is his material possessions. But we forget that when God made Himself known to Abraham, he diligently sought the Lord with all his heart and soul. It was his faithfulness to know and to obey the Lord his God that brought about Abraham's material blessings.

In the same manner Jesus, our Lord and Savior, has given us the key to success in Matthew 6:33. This key to success is repeated over and over again throughout the books of the Bible, but do we really take note of them and follow them with all our heart?

Had Abraham not believed and followed the instructions and guidelines that God gave him with all his heart, you and I would not be talking about him today.

To prove that God has given His people a hint in His word regarding keys to success, we will take a look at the same principle keys to success given to Joshua when Moses, the servant of God, died. It is written in Joshua 1:5-9:

5. *"No one will be able to stand up against you all the days of your life. As I was with Moses, so I will be with you; I will never leave you nor forsake you.*

*6. Be strong and courageous, because you will lead these people to inherit the land I swore to their forefathers to give them.*
*7. Be strong and very courageous. Be careful to obey all the law My servant Moses gave you, do not turn from it to the right or to the left, that you may be successful where ever you go.*
*8. <u>Do not let this book of the Law depart from your mouth; meditate on it day and night, so that you be careful to do everything written in it. THEN you will be prosperous and successful.</u>*
*9. Have I not commanded you? Be strong and courageous. Do not be terrified; do not be discouraged, for the Lord your God will be with you where ever you go."*

It is a well known fact that Joshua led his people, the Israelites, successfully in to the land promised them. It was because he followed diligently what the Lord his God had instructed him to do.

The question is; how do I know this as a fact?

From Joshua's own mouth, he said these words when some of the Israelites were not acting according to what the Lord had instructed them through His servant Moses. Joshua's words are recorded in chapter 24:14-15 of the book of Joshua and they read:

*14. "Now fear the Lord and serve Him with all faithfulness. Throw away the gods your forefathers worshiped beyond the river and in Egypt, and serve the Lord.*

***15. But if serving the Lord seems undesirable to you, then choose for yourselves this day whom you will serve, whether the gods your forefathers served beyond the river, or the gods of the Amorites, in whose land you are living. <u>But as for me and my household, we will serve the Lord</u>."***

Joshua knew that it was a result of serving the Lord diligently that his success became possible, and he was not going to stop serving His God as long as he was alive. Because of his success according to God's Word, he made the above underlined proclamation.

We now know that following the Word of the Almighty diligently brings success and His blessing. Abraham followed that principle and believers talk about his achievements today. We must follow Abraham's example and seek first the kingdom of God and His righteousness. Then everything will be added unto us.

God in His own loving mercy has given to us in the Bible, the same key principles for our own success and prosperity. Yet we seem not to understand any of them. We will look at some of these key principles, which are repeated in different ways over and over again in the Bible. Let us take a hard look at these scriptures and see if they are not pointing to God's blessings, which bring nothing but success and prosperity to all who follow them diligently in their lives.

Matthew 6:33 and Joshua 1:5-9 have already been quoted. Let us look at other scriptures in the Word that can lead to our success.
Psalm 1

1. *Blessed is the man who does not walk in the counsel of the wicked or stand in the way of sinners or sit in the seat of mockers.*
2. *<u>But his delight is in the law of the Lord and on His law he meditates day and night.</u>*
3. *<u>He is like a tree planted by streams of water, which yields its fruit in season and whose leaf does not wither. Whatever he does prospers.</u>*
4. *Not so the wicked! They are like chaff that the wind blows away.*
5. *Therefore the wicked will not stand in the judgment, nor sinners in the assembly of the righteous.*
6. *For the Lord watches over the way of the righteous, but the way of the wicked will perish.*

Psalm 37:7 reads, *"Delight yourself in the Lord and He will give you the desires of your heart."*
Proverbs 4:20-23 tells us:

20. *My son, pay attention to what I say; listen closely to My words.*
21. *Do not let them out of your sight, keep them within your heart*
22. *<u>For they</u>* (the words of God) *<u>are life to those who find them and health to a man's whole body</u>*

*23. Above all else, guard you heart, for it is the wellspring of life.*

In John 15:7 we read, *"If you remain in Me and My words remain in you, ask whatever you wish, and it will be given you."*

Looking at all these scripture verses, we can then ask, why is it that God seems to be repeating Himself, but in different ways?

It is for our sake that He allowed all these scriptures to be written. If perhaps we do not understand one of them, we might get the understanding through the others. It is a blessing to understand, knowing that the above scripture verses are all pointing to the same truth that leads to success.

## IN CHRIST JESUS

In the new covenant through Christ Jesus, any one who believes in Him must confess with their mouth, *"Jesus is Lord,"* and believe in their heart that God raised Him from the dead, and by one's belief and confession they are saved. That is what the scriptures in Romans 10:9-10 reveal to us:

*9. That if you confess with your mouth, "Jesus is Lord," and believe in your heart that God raised Him from the dead, you will be saved.*
*10. For it is with your heart that you believe and are justified, and it is with your mouth that you confess and are saved.*

If any one calls himself or herself a Christian and has not confessed that Jesus is Lord and believe in his or her heart that God the Father has raised Him from the dead, that person is not saved, nor can that person claim he or she is a Christian. Until that proclamation is made we are all like the people of this world without a savior.

If it is in Christ Jesus that we are new creation then we have to remain in Him with the help of the power of the Holy Spirit - no matter what happens in our world. For it is remaining in Christ Jesus that we can bear fruit. Just as Jesus reminds us in the scriptures, in John 15:4-5 which reads:

*4. "Remain in Me, and I will remain in you. No branch can bear fruit by itself; it must remain in the vine. Neither can you bear fruit unless you remain in Me.*
*5. I am the vine; you are the branches. If a man remains in Me and I remain in him, he will bear much fruit; apart from Me you can do nothing.*

Anyone who believes in Christ Jesus has to remain in Him no matter what happens in their lifetime. It is in Christ Jesus that we receive our spiritual newness. It is in Christ Jesus that we receive our right standing with God. Jesus is our righteousness. He stated this fact very clearly when He said, "*You can do nothing without Me.*"

Yes! It is true. We can do nothing without Him.

You may say you have done a lot of things without Jesus so what am I talking about?

Think about the fact that no one alive can live without breath. One can not do anything in this world without breath.

So the question is; who is the Giver of the breath of life, oh! Man of pride?

It is God who gives each and every one alive, the breath of life. Without Him we are nothing but dead bodies.

God is trinity - God the Father, God the Son, God the Holy Spirit. They are three divine persons in one God. The Bible tells us in John 1:1-5:

1. *In the beginning was the Word, and the Word was with God, and the Word was God.*
2. *He was with God in the beginning.*
3. *Through Him all things were made; without Him nothing was made that has been made.*
4. *In Him was life, and that life was the light of man.*
5. *The light shines in the darkness, but the darkness has not understood it.*

Who is the Word that the Bible is talking about?

The Word is Jesus Christ. In the beginning of creation Jesus Christ was with God. And Jesus Christ was God. It is through Jesus Christ that all things were made. Without Him nothing would have been made. Whether we accept this statement as the truth or not, the truth remains and it can not be changed.

He is the Giver of life and we can not live without Him. And again I say, whether we believe this as truth or not, that truth remains.

## THE BLOOD OF JESUS CHRIST

*"This is My blood of the covenant, which is poured out for many for the forgiveness of sins."* (Matthew 26:28)

It is through the blood of our Lord Jesus Christ that our sins have been washed away. It is through His blood that we are forgiven, and justified to come to the throne of the Almighty God in prayer. We (believers) have received our redemption through Jesus Christ's precious blood. The precious blood of our Lord Jesus Christ is still new and powerful as the day it was shed on Calvary. As the song goes; **"There is power, power wonder working power in the blood of the Lamb."**

We should not take lightly the blood of our Lord Jesus Christ. If we believe in the precious blood of the Lord, we can plead His blood or draw His blood line around us before or in time of trouble and we will surely be safe in Him.

When we have doubts and fear over what may happen to our children we can plead the blood of our Lord over and around them and believe in our heart that they are safe in the Lord's mighty hand.

When we plead the wonder working blood of Jesus over those who are under the influence of the devil, they are released. Those with broken hearts can be healed and they can live in peace. The truth is; the devil does not want to hear about the blood of Jesus Christ. And wherever the blood line is drawn, the devil will not make any attempt to go near that place. Even if he is there before, once the blood of Christ Jesus is pleaded, he flees.

As believers in Jesus Christ we have deadly weapons available to us, but we do not seem to know or understand this truth. The Lord in His mercy is begging all of His children to read, to study, and to meditate on His Word day and night, by so doing we gain knowledge. Without an understanding of the Word of God, we leave ourselves open to the deceit of the enemy, giving him the ability to steal from us and even destroy us. So let us take seriously the word of God found in the Bible and seek diligently to know all we can about our Lord and Savior. If we seek Him we will surely find Him, and know that He is the Living God. This is one of the reasons why the scripture says in Hosea 4:6, *"My people are destroyed from lack of knowledge."*

What did Jesus say about our enemy, the devil?

*"The thief comes only to steal and kill and destroy; I have come that they may have life, and have it to the full."* (John 10:10)

Jesus our Savior calls the devil a thief, and we have to know that is what the devil does best. But we can stop him from stealing from us. We can stop him from killing any member of our family before their time by getting serious with the study of the word of knowledge in the Bible. We can also stop the devil from destroying our family, our children, our marriage, our homes, and our jobs. All we have to do is to take heed of what God Almighty, the Creator of heaven and earth, has written in His Word.

Seek Him diligently through His Word. Let us delight in the Lord, and do all that He has requested of us, with all our hearts, by so doing we will be well equipped to use His precious Name, which is above all names. His name is the Sword of the Spirit [The spoken Word] that sets captives free, and His precious blood protects all that the Lord has already blessed us with and even our future blessings.

So brothers and sisters arise. Let us seek the Lord with all our hearts and souls, and surely we will see His glory on earth.

In Abraham's covenant he could not claim any power in the sacrificed animal's blood. All he could do was hold on to the Lord and the promises given to him. But as believers in Christ Jesus we can cling to the atoning blood of Christ and His name, and remain steadfast in Him.

## THE NEW COVENANT

7. *For if there had been nothing wrong with that first covenant, no place would have been sought for another.*
8. *But God found fault with the people and said: "The time is coming declares the Lord, when I will make a new covenant with the house of Israel and with the house of Judah.*
9. *<u>It will not be like the covenant I made with their</u>*

***forefathers when I took them by the hand to lead them out of Egypt, because they did not remain faithful to My covenant, and I turned away from them, declares the Lord.***
10. ***This is the covenant I will make with the house of Israel after that time declares the Lord. I will put My laws in their minds and write them on their hearts. I will be their God, and they will be My people.***
11. ***No longer will a man teach his neighbor or a man his brother, saying, "Know the Lord, because they will all know Me, from the least of them to the greatest.***
12. ***For I will forgive their wickedness and will remember their sins no more."***
13. ***By calling this covenant "new," He has made the first one obsolete, and what is obsolete and aging will soon disappear.*** (Hebrews 8:7-13)

Our new covenant in Christ Jesus is a better covenant and the blessings are extra ordinary. For it was made in the blood of God the Son Himself. There is nothing on earth better than the body of Christ and His blood, offered as atonement for our sins on the altar of the Father in heaven on our behalf. His atoning blood is better than the blood of the millions of animals, which has been offered as sacrifice for sins on earthly altars. His atoning blood is the final sacrifice for our sins; no other sacrifice is needed for God the Father to forgive sins. Jesus has done it all. Amen and Amen.

It is time for us to know this truth and start talking about our Savior and our blessings in Christ Jesus, setting our minds and goals above and beyond Abraham's blessings. This is because our Father in heaven still has better things to offer His children now and forever. We are so blessed to be alive and to know this wonderful truth. Ours is to break through the barrier of our ignorance, seek the Lord diligently, and He will, in His goodness do the rest by drawing us near to Him. He is a Father who always keeps His promises. What He says He will do, He does extra ordinarily. That is the beauty and wonder of our God.

Remember what He said through His servant Peter in 2 Peter 1:3-8:

3. *His divine power has given us everything we need for life and godliness through our knowledge of Him who called us by His own glory and goodness.*
4. *Through these He has given us His very great and precious promises, so that through them you may participate in the divine nature and escape the corruption in the world caused by evil desires.*
5. *For this very reason, make every effort to add to your faith goodness, and to goodness, knowledge.*
6. *And to knowledge, self-control; and to self-control, perseverance; and to perseverance, godliness.*

*7. And to godliness, brotherly kindness, and to brotherly kindness, love.*
*8. For if you possess these qualities in increasing measure, they will keep you from being ineffective and unproductive in your knowledge of our Lord Jesus Christ.*

The truth is in God's Word the Bible. We have to take great joy in reading and applying these truths and so remain on the path of righteousness. By God's divine power He has allowed His divine truth about life and godliness to be revealed and written down in the Holy Bible. It is for our understanding. When we allow the Holy Spirit to lead us as we study the truth in His Word, we become knowledgeable and discerning of the things which are spiritual, and so to be treated as such; and of things that are physical and to be treated as such. It is only in the Holy Bible that one can find these truths. Amen.

The Bible tells us in 2 Corinthians 5:17-19:

*17. Therefore if anyone is in Christ, he is a new creation, the old has gone, and the new has come.*
*18. All this is from God, who reconciled us to Himself through Christ and gave us the ministry of reconciliation.*
*19. That God was reconciling the world to Himself in Christ, not counting men's sins against them. And He has committed to us the message of reconciliation.*

We must remain in Christ Jesus and allow ourselves, by the work of the Holy Spirit, to become the new creation that the scriptures talk about. There is a regeneration that takes place within our spirit man as we confess the Lord Jesus Christ and the Holy Spirit seals us in His love. Through it all, God the Father in His own mercy, reunites us all to Himself through Jesus Christ.

In the same manner, through Jesus Christ, He has given all who come to Him and name His name [Jesus], the ministry of reconciliation. That means, in the very way someone witnessed to us about the gospel of Christ Jesus for us to believe, and to be saved, we are to go out into the world and do for those who have not yet believed in the gospel message of salvation.

If we do not obey and follow this first calling of our new life in Christ Jesus, it is very hard to settle in our calling. Right now, as a new creation in Christ Jesus, whenever we hear the statement, *seek ye first the kingdom of God and His righteousness*, the first thing that should come to mind is the first commission that all who are in Christ Jesus are called into.

All Christians should set a time each day to study the Word of God, if we really want to know Christ Jesus. The fact is if we do not know Christ Jesus through His Word, we can not love Him truly. For this reason I will say; **"To love Him is to know Him and to know Him is to love Him."**

For our love to be complete in Him we have to study to show ourselves approved of Him who has called us.

Jesus said in John 14:15, *"If you love Me, you will obey what I command."*

The question is how on earth will one know what He has commanded if one does not take time to study His Word?

In this age we have no excuse to say we cannot find a Bible to buy. We may have some excuses about not having the time to study the Word of God or time to pray, but do we find time to eat, to watch our favorite shows on television, to be on the phone talking about nothing with our friends?

Yes! We do have time for all these and even more, so we have no excuse whatsoever for not reading or studying the Word of God everyday.

Think about this. We have time to entertain our bodies and our souls, but concerning our spirit it seems we do not know how to take care of it. We feed this body with all kinds of good things but our spirit within we forget about. Brothers and sisters in Christ Jesus, it is time we turn around and feed our spirit with the word of God daily, praying in the power of the Holy Spirit, doing His will and obeying all His commands. That is the way we can feed our spirit within and grow spiritually.

The Bible tells us in Romans 12:3: *"Do not conform any longer to the pattern of this world, but be transformed by the renewing of your mind. <u>Then you will be able to test and approve what God's will is - His good, pleasing and perfect will."</u>*

As a new creation in Christ Jesus, He is calling us to a life of total transformation rather than to continue to live like people of the world, who are not saved. The Word of God says this transformation of not conforming to the pattern of this world will come about by renewing our mind.

With what does one renew one's mind?

One can renew one's mind by diligently studying day and night to gain understanding in the Word and to keep the Word in our heart. Also, one has to ask the Holy Spirit for understanding while studying the Word. Whatever is learned in the Bible is to be put into practice. By so doing, one does not do the things that the world demands, but what God wants and the things that are pleasing to Him. As one knows and lives by the truth of God's Word, and follows the leading of the Holy Spirit, then one is allowing the transformation or renewal of the mind.

We have read about our Lord Jesus Christ when He was living on earth and all the wonders that He did. We know that no demon could stand before Him. He had authority over them and over everything that existed in heaven and on earth. Anyone who believes in Jesus Christ has to find their place in Him and abide in Him, because we cannot bear fruit without Him. If we remain in Him and His Word remains in us, we will be successful in all that we put our hands on to do.

Imagine the authority Jesus Christ had when on earth. He healed the sick, raised the dead, cast demons out of those who were possessed. He fed the hungry, preached and taught people the way of God, turned water into wine. He gave sight to the blind and He gave the world reason to believe and turn to God, their Creator.

Imagine when Jesus Christ revealed Himself to His beloved Apostle John on the Island of Patmos. When he saw Him (Jesus), John recorded; he fell at His feet as though dead. It was because of His power in Glory.

To make this image clearer, let us read from the Apostle's own words in Revelation 1:10-18:

*10. On the Lord's Day I was in the Spirit, and I heard behind me a loud voice like a trumpet,*
*11. Which said: "Write on a scroll what you see and send it to the seven churches: to Ephesus, Smyrna, Pergamum, Thyatira, Sardis, Philadelphia and Laodicea."*
*12. I turned around to see the voice that was speaking to me. And when I turned I saw seven golden lamp stands.*
*13. Among the lamp stands was someone like a son of man, dressed in a robe reaching down to His feet and with a golden sash around His chest.*
*14. His head and hair were white like wool, as white as snow, and His eyes were like blazing fire.*
*15. His feet were like bronze glowing in a furnace, and His voice was like the sound of rushing waters.*
*16. In His right hand he held seven stars, and out of His mouth came a sharp, double edged sword. His face was like the sun shining in all its brilliance*

*17. When I saw Him, I fell at His feet as though dead. Then He placed His right hand on me and said: "Do not be afraid. I Am the First and the Last.*
*18. I Am the Living One; I was dead, and behold I Am alive for ever and ever! And I hold the keys of death and Hades."*

Now that we have some knowledge of how glorious and powerful our Lord is, whenever we are speaking of being in Him, we should know that we are also in that Glorious power as long as we remain in Him. With that confidence, let us reflect His glory on earth. Let us train our mind to picture our glorious Lord, keep within our heart this truth, and with our mouth let us proclaim the greatness of our God. Let us pray that the Holy Spirit will seal us in the Lord Jesus Christ.

To develop strong faith that we are in Jesus Christ we need to repeat and meditate on the scripture, **"Therefore, if anyone is in Christ, he is a new creation, the old has gone, the new has come!"** Then we make that scripture personal by saying; **"Right now I am in Christ Jesus. I am a new creation in Christ Jesus. The old me is gone and the new me in Christ, exists right now. I can do all things through Christ who strengthens me."** Repeating this to yourself day and night will change your outlook of things in this world, and about the kingdom's work for good.

As we grow in Christ, and His words in us grow

stronger, nothing, except ourselves, will be able to stop us. We can then walk in authority over the evil one, and take possession of all that the Lord has promised us in His Word. As our faith and our belief in the Lord Jesus grow stronger, we will be able to fulfill what Jesus said in John 14:12-14, which reads:

*12. "I tell you the truth, anyone who has faith in me will do what I have been doing. He will do even greater things than these, because I am going to the Father.*
*13. And I will do whatever you ask in My Name, so that the Son may bring glory to the Father.*
*14. You may ask me for anything in My Name, and I will do it".*

For us to be a reflection of our Lord and Savior on earth, we must believe totally in Him, remain in Him, rely and lean on His Word. He promised that if we have faith in Him and believe in Him, we will do all that He did when He was on earth. Further, we should be able to do even greater things than what He did. Those were Jesus' own words. He said this because He knew His place of authority and power with the Father. It is for the Father's glory, that whatever we ask in Jesus' name, He promised He will do it. This is something we must meditate on to truly understand. Look at it this way. The Lord of Lords who died on the cross and gave freely His blood as a ransom for our sins, is now in heaven on His throne, still interceding for us before the Father, and at the same time ready to respond to our requests in His name. Oh! What a wonderful and marvelous God we have.

There is no other god in the whole universe like our Lord Jesus Christ. He is the living God who has the unfailing love to do all that He did for us and is still doing on our behalf. Praise and honor be to His holy name, Jesus Christ. Amen.

As we continue to read His word, pray and obey Him, all that we desire and even that for which we do not ask, will be added onto us. Long life, good health, joy and peace are only some of the good things that God promised to us.

## DO NOT GO BACK

Now that you have been redeemed from the jaws of the darkness of sin and have been called into the light of God, do not by any means go back doing those things that you were redeemed out of, when you were in the world of darkness. By now we all know how God called Abraham to come out of his country, away from his people and from his father's household. This process is just as if he was called from the world of darkness into God's light, where God Himself was to direct his path.

When Abraham reached the land where God wanted him to be, the Bible tells us that Almighty God appeared to Abraham, to confirm His promise that He would give that land to Abraham's offspring.

Abraham even built an altar in praise of Almighty God, who had appeared to him in that land of promise.

Shortly after that time, a severe famine hit the land. Abraham decided to go to Egypt rather than remain in the land where God had called him to be. That was a mistake. For Abraham did not go to God in prayer first, seeking the counsel of the Lord who had called him into that land of promise, to ask for His direction in that difficult moment.

Abraham missed the mark by taking it upon himself to make his own decision by his own counsel. Abraham had no excuse not to go to God for His counsel, because Abraham had the ability to hear from God. Yes! He did hear from God. That was how he knew to come to the land of promise. Even when he reached the land, it is recorded that Almighty God appeared to him and talked with him. Let us read that story from Genesis 12:5-7:

5. *He took his wife Sarai, his nephew Lot, all the possessions they had accumulated and the people they had acquired in Haran, and they set out for the land of Canaan, and they arrived there.*
6. *Abram traveled through the land as far as the site of the great tree of Moreh at Shechem. At that time the Canaanites were in the land.*
7. *The Lord appeared to Abram and said, "To your offspring I will give this land." So he built an altar there to the Lord, who had appeared to him.*

As the truth has been revealed from the Bible, what could possibly have been his reason for not going to God first, before packing everything that he brought with him from the land of his birth, and head to Egypt?

We who are saved should know that the devil always attacks us through suggestions to our minds, putting fear in our hearts. Any time we yield to his suggestions and the fear that he brings, we surely will miss our steps on the path of righteousness. What he does is draw us away from the protection of God into his world of confusion so that he can derail us from the will of God.

I believe the devil crippled Abraham with suggestions of fear of losing everything he had. Then he (Abraham), in his fear, took action to save himself and all his possessions. By so doing, he fell out of the protection of God, right into the arms of the evil one. We can also say that through his fear, the devil was able to lead Abraham into a place he controls, where he could try to undo what God the Almighty had spoken into Abraham's life.

You know, when our eyes are full of tears we can not see clearly and it might cause us to stumble if we try to walk, in the same way when we are fearful and we try to make hasty decisions without seeking God first, we are surely going to make mistakes that we will regret later on in life. So it is always the right thing to do, to seek God first in everything, all the time.

We, who are saved through Christ Jesus, should

pay attention to what our God who is the creator of all creation is telling us about not being fearful because, He has not given us the spirit of fear, but a spirit of power and a sound mind. The one who brings about the spirit of fear is the devil.

Remember fear is a spirit (evil spirit) and we should not give him a chance in our lives. The only spirit we should allow in our lives is the Holy Spirit from our God.

Although it is not recorded that the devil attacked Abraham with fear, with revelation, I understand this truth. It was on the way to Egypt that the devil increased his attack by putting so much fear in Abraham's mind, leading Abraham to believe that he would be killed in Egypt because of the beauty of his wife. That is why Abraham told Sarah to inform any one wanting to know their relationship, that she was his sister.

What was the reason behind this attack?

The devil realized that it would be through Abraham and Sarah that the nation of God would come, and some thing good would surely come out of that. The devil did not really know all that God had in His mind for Abraham and his children. For that reason, the devil made up his evil mind that he would thwart whatever it was that God had in mind for Abraham and his wife. Causing Abraham, in fear, to call Sarah his sister instead of his wife, would free a foreigner to take Sarah for himself. In that way, God's promise would be nullified. It was the devil's aim to destroy the plan of God. Abraham yielded to the devil's plan without knowing what he was doing.

Take note of this truth; whatever the devil had suggested to Abraham's mind that brought fear, Abraham spoke out in his own words; and, it did happen the very way he had feared, as soon as they entered the land of Egypt. Let us read what is recorded in Genesis 12:10-20:

*10. Now there was a famine in the land and Abram went down to Egypt to live there for a while because the famine was severe.*

*11. As he was about to enter Egypt, he said to his wife Sarai, "I know what a beautiful woman you are.*

*12. When the Egyptians see you, they will say, 'This is his wife. Then they will kill me but will let you live.*

*13. Say you are my sister, so that I will be treated well for your sake and my life will be spared because of you."*

*14. When Abram came to Egypt, the Egyptians saw that she was a very beautiful woman.*

*15. And when Pharaoh's officials saw her, they praised her to Pharaoh, and she was taken into his palace.*

*16. He treated Abram well for her sake, and Abram acquired sheep and cattle, male and female donkeys, menservants and <u>maidservants,</u> and camels.*

*17. But the Lord inflicted serious diseases on*

*Pharaoh and his household because of Abram's wife Sarai.*
***18.****So Pharaoh summoned Abram. "What have you done to me?" he said. "Why didn't you tell me she was your wife?*
***19.****Why did you say, 'She is my sister,' so that I took her to be my wife? Now then, here is your wife. Take her and go!"*
***20.****Then Pharaoh gave orders about Abram to his men, and they sent him on his way, with his wife and everything he had.*

Note that our Lord Jesus Christ has given us this truth in His word, *"I tell you the truth, if anyone says to this mountain; 'Go throw yourself into the sea,' and does not doubt in his heart but believes that what he says will happen, it will be done for him."* (Mark 11:23)

The devil is using that same principle of God in reverse, he knows that whatever you fear the most in your heart, and think of, and say with your own mouth, he (the devil) will see to it that it happens to you the same way that fear was imaged. That is the reason why the Lord continually tells us in His word, "Do not be afraid." For fear will surely derail us from the will of God. Be careful what comes out of your mouth, for you will surely eat the fruit of it. Now that the truth is revealed, let us continue with our study of what happened to Abraham.

In Abraham's case we have seen that everything that he had feared all came to pass in the same way he saw it in his mind and spoke it. His wife had been taken; he had been showered with all kinds of gifts in exchange. That means he had relinquished to the devil, on a silver platter, God's call on his life - without even knowing this fact.

At this point, because God was not willing to see his plan for the future delayed, He (God) intervened. He inflicted diseases on Pharaoh, and his household, for taking Sarah as his wife. God did not hide what He was doing from Pharaoh. He made known the cause of the diseases. Pharaoh could not fight God. He returned Abraham's wife and ordered Abraham to leave his country. In all this, Abraham came back to the very place he had run away from.

Although we may say he escaped unharmed from the hands of the devil with God's plan still intact, still, damage had been done within.

Do you remember the gifts and possessions Abraham acquired (verse 16, in the scriptures above?). Among those, he acquired the maid servant Hagar. She was the enemy planted within. You see now that the first plan of the devil failed, but he had his second plan in place to follow up at a later day. Through the maid servant Hagar, the devil would continue trying to derail God's plan. This second plan of the devil worked for a time, but in the end it failed, because of the love God has for mankind. God has always determined to redeem man whom He made in His own image and likeness.

It is through the descendants of Abraham that Christ our Savior was to come, to fulfill God's promise of love to His children which we know today as, ***"For God so loved the world that He gave His one and only Son that whoever believes in Him shall not perish but have eternal life."*** (John 3:16)

It is only by the power of God's love and His merciful kindness that Abraham had his breakthrough to success. God knew the heart of Abraham. He knew Abraham had a heart of obedience and that he was willing and determined to do whatever God wanted him to do no matter what happened. God always rewards obedient hearts. He tells us in the scriptures, ***"If you are willing and obedient, you will eat the best from the land; but if you resist and rebel, you will be devoured by the sword."*** (Isaiah 1:19-20)

Now, let all who name the name of the Lord Jesus Christ be careful, and mindful not to go back to the worldly things that we have been redeemed from. Let us not even look back at those filthy behaviors that we have turned away from. For God in His loving kindness has made it known to us in His own words, ***"Forget the former things; do not dwell on the past."***

Why would God say these words if they were not true?

If we continually look back and go back to the former things, we will fall into the trap of the evil one, and we will not be able to enjoy God's unfailing love fully. Further, if we continue going back and forth in our sin, nonbelievers will see what we do and our actions will bring nothing but disgrace to the name of our Lord Jesus Christ. At the end it will be as if we are crucifying Jesus over and over again.

We would never choose to bring any disgrace to the name of the Lord if we fully know what He has done for us and what He continues to do for you and me in heaven. Let us not take His sacrificial death on the cross for our sins for granted. Let us in everyway cherish His redeeming love by being fully committed to obey everything that He has commanded us to do. Let us try our best to remain in His love always, through our dedication to prayer, study of the scriptures and loving one another at all times, for the rest of our days on earth till our Lord comes back.

Let us pray for the Lord to open up our eyes to see the things He has done for us, the things He has in His heart to keep on doing for us. Know this for sure, He is doing totally new things in our lives, because He said in His own words, *"See I am doing a new thing! Now it springs up, do you not perceive it? I am making a way in the desert and streams in the wasteland.*

*The wild animals honor Me, the jackals and the owls, because I provide water in the desert and streams in the wasteland, to give drink to My people, My chosen. The people I formed for Myself that they may proclaim My praise.* (Isaiah 43:19-21)

From these scriptures, we see that God the Father of all creation has not forgotten us, His creation. His promises are always true. He will always do what He has spoken in His word of promise. It is always up to us whether we will allow His promises to be fulfilled in our lives or not. If we are willing and obedient to do all that He has commanded in His Word, then we shall enjoy all that He has promised and eat the good of the land.

So let us do first things first. Seek His kingdom and His righteousness, then everything, every blessing in His promise, the Holy Bible, will be ours, overtaking us wherever we may be in this world.

Remember this always. What we know now, Abraham did not know. Yet he trusted his God and God honored his trust by calling Abraham His friend. We know much more about God now than did those before us, so let us use the time we have, and understand we are His people. God loves us, and formed us for Him-self, that we should sing His praise now and for ever more. It is there and then that we can be a blessing in the kingdom of God on earth.

The kingdom of God on earth is lacking so much, because the ones, who are to receive their blessings in order to bless the kingdom, are not making the effort to read or study the word of God, to know the truth, and live by the truth. In so doing they do not understand or know what they are to do in order to receive their blessings and in return, bless the kingdom of God on earth.

Even those who do study do not practice what they know. It is time to arise and take what is yours from the devil, for Jesus Christ has won the victory on the cross, by His sacrificial death on your behalf. Obey all He has commanded, and you shall be blessed beyond the blessings that we know - spiritually, physically and materially.

Remember, we have all the opportunity in the world, through Christ Jesus, to go beyond Abraham's blessings and enter into the blessings of Christ Jesus. For it is in His image that we are being conformed. In all this, we are more than conquerors through Jesus who loves us dearly.

It is when you are blessed that you can fully be a blessing in His kingdom. Then the kingdom message will be able to reach every corner of the earth. Amen.

# CHAPTER 2

# THE HOLY SPIRIT

God is one. He is the Creator of heaven and the earth. He created everything in heaven and on earth. There are three divine persons in God which is called the Trinity; God the Father, God the Son, and God the Holy Spirit. Each divine person is fully God.

## THE WORK OF THE HOLY SPIRIT

The Holy Spirit is the third divine person of the trinity. He is fully God. The work of the Holy Spirit has been in existence since the Old Testament. But His works then were limited only to specially chosen people that God wanted to use, such as the prophets, rulers (kings), priests or anyone, at a particular moment, who God wanted to use for His own glory.

In the Old Testament it is known that Moses was

filled with the power of the Holy Spirit. When leading the children of Israel was becoming difficult for Moses and he complained before God, God asked Moses to choose seventy elders upon whom He (God) would place a portion of the Spirit that was upon Moses, so that these chosen men would be able to help Moses lead the people. This truth can be found in Numbers 11:14-17 and it reads:

**14.** *I cannot carry all these people by myself; the burden is too heavy for me.*
**15.** *If this is how you are going to treat me, put me to death right now if I have found favor in your eyes and do not let me face my own ruin.*
**16.** *The Lord said to Moses; "Bring Me seventy of Israel's elders who are known to you as leaders and official among the people. Have them come to the Tent of meeting that they may stand there with you.*
**17.** *I will come down and speak with you there and I will take of the Spirit that is on you and put the Spirit in them. They will help you carry the burden of the people so that you will not have to carry it alone."*

Moses did as God told him. When the time came for all of them to be present at the Tent of meeting, two of the chosen elders were not there along with the rest of them. God met them as promised and filled them with His Spirit, even the two elders who were not present but remained in their tents. We can still read this record of this truth in Numbers 11:24-30:

*24. So Moses went out and told the people what the Lord had said. He brought together seventy of their elders and had them stand around the Tent.*
*25. Then the Lord came down in the cloud and spoke with him, and He took of the Spirit that was on him and put the Spirit on the seventy elders. When the Spirit rested on them, they prophesied, but they did not do so again.*
*26. However, two men, whose names were Eldad and Medad, had remained in the camp. They were listed among the elders but did not go out to the Tent. Yet the Spirit also rested on them, and they prophesied in the camp.*
*27. A young man ran and told Moses, "Eldad and Medad are prophesying in the camp."*
*28. Joshua son of Nun, who had been Moses' aide since youth, spoke up and said, "Moses, my lord, stop them!"*
*29. But Moses replied, "Are you jealous for my sake? I wish that, all the Lord's people were prophets and that the Lord would put His Spirit on them!"*
*30. Then Moses and the elders of Israel returned to the camp.*

The Holy Spirit is the empowering power for all whom the Lord has called into His service. Anyone who is to be effectively used by the Lord needs to be filled with the Holy Spirit. That was the case of the seventy elders called to serve with Moses. The Holy Spirit, who is the anointing Spirit of God, anointed the seventy chosen elders for God's work, and they were able help Moses carry the burden of the people.

The Holy Spirit is also called the Counselor. He counsels God's people. He is the Spirit of truth who guides all believers into the truth of God, if we allow Him to. He is the seal of guarantee that we are the children of God. He is the Comforter and a Helper in times of need.

It is also recorded in the Bible that when the people of Israel wanted a king to rule over them instead of God, the first king was chosen and he was filled with the Holy Spirit. His life changed from that day forth. From the reading in the Bible of 1 Samuel 10:8-11, Samuel the prophet gave Saul instructions. When he followed the instructions he was given, Saul, chosen to be the first king of Israel, was anointed into the office of king by the Holy Spirit.

8. *"Go down ahead of me to Gilgal. I will surely come down to you to sacrifice burnt offerings and fellowship offerings, but you must wait seven days until I come to you and tell you what you are to do."*
9. *As Saul turned to leave Samuel, God changed Saul's heart, and all these signs were fulfilled that day.*
10. *When they arrived at Gibeah, a procession*

*of prophets met him; the Spirit of God came upon him in power, and he joined in their prophesying.*
*11. When all those who had formerly known him saw him prophesying with the prophets, the asked each other, "What is this that has happened to the son of Kish? Is Saul also among the prophets?"*

Now we have seen from the two Old Testament books of the Bible that we have read. When the Holy Spirit came upon the ones whom God called to His service, there was always a sign or evidence that they were anointed by the power of the Holy Spirit. There is always a show of God's power and evidence of prophesy.

It is very important for us to come to know more about the Holy Spirit. In the very way that Jesus Christ was promised to the world from the beginning, to be the one to bring salvation to mankind, the Holy Spirit has been promised to all who would believe in God the Father through Jesus Christ. It is in Joel 2:28-29, that the Holy Spirit was promised.

*28. And afterward, I will pour out My Spirit on all people. Your sons and daughters will prophesy, your old men will dream dreams, your young men will see visions.*
*29. Even on My servants, both men and women, I will pour out My Spirit in those days.*

Are those days, promised by the Lord, past?

Yes! The day that God was talking about is far gone. The Holy Spirit has been poured out, and whosoever wants to receive the infilling of the Spirit has only to ask God for that infilling, and it will be done.

*"If you then, though you are evil, know how to give good gifts to your children, how much more will your Father in heaven give the Holy Spirit to those who ask Him?"* (Luke 11:13)

We have to desire the Holy Spirit. Remember, He will not force Himself on anyone. He comes freely to those who desire Him in their hearts. It is very important for all who love, and believe in God the Almighty, to receive the infilling of the Holy Spirit. For the Holy Spirit has been poured on earth for our sake.

If someone comes to you as a believer, and asks, "Do you love the Lord Jesus Christ?" what will your answer be? It will surely be, yes, without a second thought. That will surely be the answer for all those who believe in Christ Jesus. But what did our Lord say about those who love Him?

Jesus said in His own words: *"If you love Me, you will obey what I command."* (John 14:15)

Now that we know what He said, let us put our love for Christ to the test by taking a good look at His words of commission in Mark 16:14-18, and see if we are doing the things that He has commanded us to do.

*14. Later Jesus appeared to the Eleven as they were eating; He rebuked them for their lack of faith and their stubborn refusal to believe those who had seen Him after He had risen.*
*15. He said to them, "Go into all the world and preach the good news to all creation.*
*16. Whoever believes and is baptized will be saved, but whoever does not believe will be condemned.*
*17. And these signs will accompany those who believe. In My name they will drive out demons; <u>they will speak in new tongues.</u>*
*18. They will pick up snakes with their hands, and when they drink deadly poison, it will not hurt them at all, they will place their hands on sick people, and they will get well."*

Jesus Christ said these signs shall follow those who believe. But before those who believe in Him can experience the signs named above, we who are commissioned to go into the world have to first experience these signs in our lives. If not, we are going into the world empty handed.

First of all, we who are saved have to go through the process of being saved; that is, confessing Jesus Christ as Lord of our lives as it is written in Romans 10:9-10.

All believers have to be water baptized in Christ Jesus, for this symbolizes our baptism into His death and resurrection. Just as Christ was raised from the dead through the glory of the Father, we, too, may live a new life in Him. (Romans 6) This water baptism is not the sprinkling of water but immersion into a pool of water.

When one dies, he or she is buried in a grave. In the same way, during water baptism in a pool, the water becomes our grave, where we are buried and then raised from our death and burial, into our resurrection in Christ Jesus. It is very important that all Christians who are in Christ Jesus go through water baptism, just as Christ went through Himself in order to show us how important water baptism is. If one is a Christian one can not say he or she does not believe in water baptism, but must remember it is part of the package of being in Christ Jesus.

All who believe in Christ Jesus have been given the authority to take dominion over everything on earth, including the devil. That is why we who are in Christ Jesus have the power of Christ to drive or cast out demons.

Believers have the divine authority in Christ Jesus to pray and lay hands on the sick, in the name of Jesus, for the sick to be healed. This is because the Bible tells us in 1 Peter 2:24: *"**He Himself bore our sins in His body on the tree, so that we might die to sins and live for righteousness; by His wounds you have been healed.**"*

If we have been healed since the day Jesus was beaten, wounded, and crucified on our behalf, then healing is ours by right in Christ Jesus. However, by walking on snakes and drinking deadly poison, the Word of God is not telling believers to go about playing with snakes or drinking deadly poisons. What the word of God is implying is that if by accident, one who believes in Christ Jesus picks up a snake or drinks a poison, he or she will not be hurt.

Apostle Paul had a face-to-face encounter with a viper and he was not hurt. It is recorded in Acts 28:1-6; and it reads:

1. *Once safely on shore, we found out that the island was called Malta.*
2. *The islanders showed us unusual kindness. They built a fire and welcomed us all because it was raining and cold.*
3. *Paul gathered a pile of brushwood and as he put it on the fire, a viper driven out by the heat, fastened itself on his hand.*
4. *When the islanders saw the snake hanging from his hand, they said to each other, 'This man must be a murderer, for though he escaped from the sea, Justice has not allowed him to live.'*
5. *But Paul shook the snake off into the fire <u>and suffered no ill effects.</u>*
6. *The people expected him to swell up or suddenly fall dead, but after waiting a long time and seeing nothing unusual happen to him, they changed their minds and said he was a god.*

Paul's experience on the island is very clear and we know that God's words are always true.

## THE NEW TONGUES

About the unknown tongue, we Christians have to pray for the Holy Spirit to help us understand what it really is. As seen in the Old Testament, the tongue has always been there. Though not identified as tongue, it was there as a part of prophesy. Then in the New Testament it was identified and distinguished as both tongue and prophesy.

Jesus, who is the Lord of all mankind, knows what happens when the Holy Spirit comes on man. So, in His word of commission He spoke about believers speaking in new tongues.

After Jesus Christ resurrected, He told His disciples to wait in Jerusalem for the Holy Spirit, as written in Acts 1:4-8:

*4. On one occasion, while He was eating with them, He gave them this command: "Do not leave Jerusalem, but wait for the gift My Father promised, which you have heard Me speak about.*
*5. For John baptized with water, but in a few days you will be baptized with the Holy Spirit."*
*6. So when they met together, they asked Him, "Lord, are you at this time going to restore the kingdom to Israel?"*
*7. He said to them: "It is not for you to know the times or dates the Father has set by His own authority.*
*8. But you will receive power when the Holy Spirit comes on you, and you will be witnesses in Jerusalem, and in all Judea and Samaria, and*

# GOING BEYOND ABRAHAM'S BLESSING

*to the ends of the earth."*

The disciples waited as they were commanded by the Lord, and on the day of Pentecost the Holy Spirit fell upon them. This is what is recorded in Acts 2:1-4:

1. *When the day of Pentecost came, they were all together in one place.*
2. *Suddenly a sound like the blowing of a violent wind came from heaven and filled the whole house where they were sitting.*
3. *<u>They saw what seemed to be tongues of fire that separated and came to rest on each of them.</u>*
4. *<u>All of them were filled with the Holy Spirit and began to speak in other tongues as the Spirit enabled them.</u>"*

On the day of Pentecost, God's promise both in the Old and the New Testament was fulfilled when the Holy Spirit was poured on earth. He came pouring in as a mighty wind from heaven, with tongues of fire, which the disciples of the Lord saw, resting on each ones' head. It was there and then that they were all filled with the Holy Spirit and spoke in tongues as the Lord Jesus has stated in His word of commission. From that time on, the tongues has become the physical evidence of receiving the Holy Spirit.

When the disciples of the Lord first received the Holy Spirit and speaking in tongues, nonbelievers outside heard them and knew something was going on with those disciples. The same way, as reported in the Old Testament with the seventy elders Moses had chosen, and when Saul was called to be the first king and he met the prophets on his way, the Holy Spirit came upon them. These men were filled with the same Holy Spirit, and spoke in tongues; and though in the Old Testament tongues were not yet identified, prophesy were. Later on, in the New Testament, tongues were clearly identified by what Jesus said in the words of commission, and what the disciples saw with their own eyes as tongues of fire resting on the disciples' heads while they spoke in tongues. Even other people heard them speak new tongues.

With this proof, who are we to say it is not true, or it is not for us today? Can we claim we love the Lord if we refuse all these manifestations in our lives? How can we go into the world and be good witnesses for God if we reject the power of the Holy Spirit, who will make us better witnesses?

It is totally impossible to go in to the world to preach Christ Jesus and for these signs and wonders that He claimed in His word of commission to follow us if we simply refuse to obey His commands, even if only in part. Let each one of us in Christ check our hearts to see if we are in obedience to the Lord when it comes to receiving the in filling of the Holy Spirit. If we have received the infilling of the Holy Spirit with evidence of speaking in tongues, God bless us. But if we check and we know in our hearts that we have not been filled with the Holy Spirit, with the evidence of speaking in tongues, we should not be ashamed or afraid to ask God. Go to a church that knows about the Holy Spirit and ask to know more of the Holy Spirit. Then ask them to pray for you to receive the Holy Spirit.

I will tell of something that happened between a group of Christians and me in Malawi. When I met one person from this particular group, we talked about Christ Jesus and the Holy Spirit. During that time she made it known to me that their leader told them they received the infilling of the Holy Spirit when they became believers in Christ Jesus. So I asked her to tell me about the Holy Spirit, but she could not tell me anything about the Spirit of God. What she did was to invite me to their Bible study.

After the Bible study, and when it was time for questions and answers, I put up my hand and asked if they had received the power of the Holy Spirit since they believed, just as Paul had asked the believers at Ephesus, when he met them for the first time. The leader was very quick to answer, saying they had all received the infilling of the Holy Spirit. I asked him to prove it to me. He quickly turned to Ephesians 1:13-14, and read:

*13. And you also were included in Christ when you heard the word of truth, the gospel of your salvation. Having believed, you were marked in Him with a seal, the promised Holy Spirit.*
*14. Who is a deposit guaranteeing our inheritance until the redemption of those who are God's possession to the praise of His glory.*

I begged him to please stop, before we confuse the people. I asked him to read the first verse of the chapter that he just read, which indicated that what he was reading was Paul's letter to believers in Ephesus. I told the leader and the group, I could not write a letter to a group of people if I do not know them, so if Paul had written a letter to these believers, which we are now reading, then Paul must have already met them and known their spiritual state of mind. Then later on, when he was away from them he wrote to encourage them to remain faithful to their call.

I told them that for us to really understand and know what Paul was talking about in verse 13, we must find out about the first the time Paul met these believers, and find out what happened then and later on, and why he was writing such a letter to them. I asked if we could turn to Act 19:1-7. It reads:

1. *While Apollos was at Corinth, Paul took the road through the interior and arrived at Ephesus. There he found some disciples*
2. *And asked them, "Did you receive the Holy Spirit when you believed?" They answered, "No we have not even heard that there is a Holy Spirit."*
3. *So Paul asked, "Then what baptism did you receive?" "John's baptism," they replied.*
4. *Paul said, "John's baptism was a baptism of repentance. He told the people to believe in the One coming after him, that is, in Jesus."*

**5. On hearing this, they were baptized into the name of the Lord Jesus.
6. When Paul placed his hands on them, the Holy Spirit came on them, and they spoke in tongues and prophesied.
7. There were about twelve men in all.**

When the above scripture was read, we all knew then what had happened between Paul and the believers, when they met for the first time. Paul asked them one of the very important questions in Christianity, asked after going through the prayer of salvation. Have you received the Holy Spirit when you believed? These believers spoke the truth to Paul and he helped them understand the truth. Then he prayed and laid his hands on them, and they were filled with the Holy Spirit.

The question is, how did he know they then received the Holy Spirit?

The truth is that they all spoke in tongues and prophesied. That was the evidence of being filled with the Holy Spirit, and Paul knew this as a fact.

After giving the group this truth, I then asked them again if they had received the Holy Spirit. Some responded they had not. Some said that they did not know. The rest did not want to disappoint their leader so they said yes; they had already received the Holy Spirit. The question then becomes, are we trying to please man or God? If we are trying to please man, and put our trust in man, we have to be very careful, for God said in His own Word, in Jeremiah 17:5-8:

5. *This is what the Lord says: "Cursed is the one who trusts in man, who depends on flesh for his strength and whose heart turns away from the Lord.*
6. *He will be like a bush in the wastelands; he will not see prosperity when it comes. He will dwell in the parched places of the desert, in a salt land where no one lives.*
7. *But blessed is the man who trusts in the Lord, whose confidence is in Him.*
8. *He will be like a tree planted by the water that sends out its roots by the stream. It does not fear when heat comes; its leaves are always green. It has no worries in a year of drought and never fails to bear fruit.*

For us to be fruitful in the kingdom of God we have to trust God, through His Word, the Bible. If anyone tells us something that is not centered on the Word of God and wants us to obey or take his or her word as the truth, I advise you take off and run for your dear life, for God says cursed is the one who trusts in man.

God should be the One whom we trust, but how can we trust God the Almighty if we do not take time off from our busy life to study the Word of God? How then can we know the truth from a lie? It is a good thing to study the Word of God daily, and to pray daily in order to build trust and that wonderful fellowship with our God.

Let us go back to Apostle Paul. One may ask, what

did he know about the Holy Spirit, because he was not there at the beginning when the disciples were filled on the day of Pentecost. We should not forget, when Paul was called, Ananias was sent to pray for him to see again, and for him to be filled with the Holy Spirit, Acts`9. There is no record that Paul spoke in tongues when he received the Holy Spirit, but I know for sure he did speak in tongues as the Spirit lead him. It's because Paul himself gave a testimony saying; **"I thank God that I speak in tongues more than all of you."** (1 Corinthians 14:18)

Now that we know what Paul said, because he knew that speaking in tongues is the evidence of being filled with the Holy Spirit, we also know that Paul would ask any believer if they have received the Spirit of truth, knowing the evidence that follows.

Let us look at a new evidence of the Holy Spirit and certain new believers in Christ Jesus. During a great persecution against the church at Jerusalem, the apostles scattered throughout Judea and Samaria. Philip went down to Samaria and preached the good news to the people of Samaria. This reading can be found in Acts 8:12- 21:

*12.But when they believed Philip as he preached the good news of the kingdom of God and the name of Jesus Christ, they were baptized, both men and women.*
*13.Simon himself believed and was baptized. And he followed Philip everywhere, astonished by the great signs and miracles he saw.*

*14. When the apostles in Jerusalem heard that Samaria had accepted the word of God, they sent Peter and John to them.*
*15. When they arrived, they prayed for them that they might receive the Holy Spirit.*
*16. Because the Holy Spirit had not yet come upon any of them, they had simply been baptized into the name of the Lord Jesus.*
*17. Then Peter and John placed their hands on them, and they received the Holy Spirit.*
*18. When Simon saw that the Spirit was given at the laying on of the apostles' hands, he offered them money.*
*19. And said, "Give me also this ability so that everyone on whom I lay my hands may receive the Holy Spirit."*
*20. Peter answered: "May your money perish with you, because you thought you could buy the gift of God with money.*
*21. You have no part or share in the ministry, because your heart is not right before God.*

In this chapter, we see clearly how when Philip preached the good news of our Lord Jesus Christ to the men and women of Samaria, they believed the gospel which is the good news, and they were baptized just like we have gone through ourselves.

The Bible tells us, when the good news was preached and they opened their hearts and received the word of God they were baptized, the signs and wonders promised in Jesus' word of commission came to pass. Here the Bible tells us, when the apostles in Jerusalem heard that the men and women of Samaria had opened their hearts to the word of God, they sent to them Peter and John. Why did they have to send these two to them who have accepted Jesus Christ as their Savior and were even baptized in water? The answer is very clear in verses 15 to 17; it is because the Holy Spirit had not yet come upon anyone of them. The Bible puts it simply; *"They had simply been baptized into the name of the Lord Jesus."*

They had to pray for them and lay hands on them to receive the Holy Spirit and speak in tongues just as Peter, John and other disciples of the Lord did on the day of Pentecost. We all know how it happened on the day of Pentecost. Peter and John were live witnesses to that truth.

At yet another time, in Acts chapter 10, Peter was compelled to go to Joppa to meet a Gentile, Cornelius, and his family, to minister to them the good news of Christ Jesus. During the cause of his preaching the Holy Spirit came upon them. When he went back to Jerusalem to give a report of what had happened, the rest of the apostles did not believe that could happen to Gentiles also, so Peter in his own words said, *"As I began to speak, the Holy Spirit came on them as He had come on us at the beginning. Then I remembered what the Lord had said: 'John baptized with water, but you will be baptized with the Holy Spirit.' So if God gave them the same gift as He gave us, who believed in the Lord Jesus*

*Christ, who was I to think that I could oppose God?"* (Acts 11:15-17)

Those words were Peter's confession of the truth, so if there is a pastor, or evangelist, or what ever name they may bear, who tells us otherwise, then there is no truth in them. You see, God knows why He has to give us the Holy Spirit with the evidence of new tongues. We can try to use our little minds to justify what God is doing but we will never come close to the truth. Some of the reasons why we must humble ourselves to receive the infilling of Holy Spirit of God are made plain in the Word of God, the Bible. They are as follows:

*"For any one who speaks in a tongue does not speak to men but to God. Indeed, no one understands him; he utters mysteries with his spirit."* (1 Corinthians 14:2)

*"In the same way, the Spirit helps us in our weakness. We do not know what we out to pray for, but the Spirit Himself intercedes for us with groans that words cannot express. And He who searches our hearts knows the mind of the Spirit, because the Spirit intercedes for the saints in accordance with God's will."* (Romans 8:26-27)

*"And pray in the Spirit on all occasions with all kinds of prayers and requests. With this in mind, be alert and always keep on praying for all the saints."* (Ephesians 6:18)

*"But you, dear friends, build yourselves up in your most holy faith and pray in the Holy Spirit."* (Jude 20)

*"Yet a time is coming <u>and has now come when the true worshipers will worship the Father in Spirit and truth, for they are the kind of worshipers the Father seeks. God is Spirit, and His worshipers must worship in Spirit and in truth.</u>"* (John 4:23-24)

*"He who speaks in a tongue edifies himself, but he who prophesies edifies the church."* (1 Corinthians 14:4)

Jesus made it very plain in the book of John that a time is coming, and has come, when the true worshipers will worship the Father in Spirit and in truth. This is the time He was speaking about, the time that the Father could pour the Holy Spirit out on all flesh who are willing to open up their hearts to ask the Father for the infilling of the Holy Spirit.

God the Father wants all His children to have wonderful fellowship with Him, as sinners saved through Christ Jesus. He knows how desperately we human beings need the Holy Spirit to make complete our understanding of His divine nature. To know the truth of God's finished work and to strengthen our fellowship with the Father are the reasons why He said in John 16:7-15:

7. *But I tell you the truth: It is for your good that I am going away. Unless I go away, the Counselor will not come to you; but if I go, I will send Him to you.*
8. *When He comes, He will convict the world of guilt in regard to sin and righteousness and judgment:*

9. *In regard to sin, because men do not believe in Me.*
10. *In regard to righteousness, because I am going to the Father, where you can see Me no longer.*
11. *And in regard to judgment, because the prince of this world now stands condemned*
12. *I have much more to say to you, more than you can now bear.*
13. *But when He, the Holy Spirit of truth, comes, He will guide you into all truth. He will not speak on His own, He will speak only what He hears, and He will tell you what is yet to come.*
14. *He will bring glory to Me by taking from what is mine and making it known to you.*
15. *All that belongs to the Father is mine. That is why I said the Spirit will take from what is mine and make it known to you.*

God in His own wisdom knows how the Trinity works and He has commanded us to receive the Holy Spirit. As servants of God, we should not fight God, but humble ourselves and receive the infilling of the Holy Spirit. For us to be efficient in our service to our Lord, we all need the infilling power of the Holy Spirit to be able to overcome the works of the evil one, who is always working against the kingdom of God. For the word of God says, ***"But you will receive power when the Holy Spirit comes on you; and you will be my witnesses in Jerusalem, and in all Judea and Samaria, and to the ends of the earth."*** (Acts 1:8)

The early disciples have done their witnessing. Now, we believers in Christ Jesus have the whole world in front of us. Before the Lord comes we have to reach every corner of the world. There is no way we can reach every corner of the world in our own strength. As it is recorded in the Bible, *"It is not by might, nor by power, but by my Spirit," says the Lord Almighty."*

The word of the Lord has revealed the truth to us that we cannot do the work of the Lord thinking we could use our own strength and power. If we think that way, we will surely fail. But if we entrust our lives into the mighty hands of the Lord and receive the infilling of the Holy Spirit, and continually pray in the Holy Spirit, we will grow spiritually. We will be used mightily by God for His glory, for the fact that we will not be using our own strength but depending fully on the power of the Holy Spirit.

This is a true story. When I was in Malawi (central Africa), a mother brought her son to be prayed for because he had been demon possessed for a long time. The pastor set a day for the boy to be brought in for his deliverance, in the name of Jesus. Before he was brought in, we fasted and prayed in the Holy Spirit diligently for the Lord to use us for His own glory.

On that faithful day I was chosen to assist the pastor. We began to pray and cast out the demons from the boy.

You have to realize that the group of Christians with whom I was then serving the Lord, had the manifestation of all the gifts of the Holy Spirit at work. As prayer went forth, those with the gift of visions saw demons fleeing. Then suddenly, from the boy's own mouth came these words, "We are all gone." His words were supporting the visions and messages that we had received.

The pastor then said, "Let us all thank the Lord for they are all gone." I immediately took the pastor aside and asked him, "Who is speaking through the boy?" He realized then that the demons were playing their dirty tricks, but could not fool all of us, as we were united in Christ Jesus. I requested if he would ask those with fear in their hearts, because of the way the boy was behaving, to leave the room where the prayer was taking place. When this request was presented the room almost emptied. Only a handful was left.

As soon as we gathered around the boy to pray and cast out what was left in the him, he suddenly got up ( he had been kneeling down) and came to me face to face, with his eyes red, and said with authority, "You, who you are?" I replied with authority and said, "I am a servant of Jesus Christ. I am here to cast you out." As soon as I said that, he turned to the pastor and asked him the same question, to which the pastor repeated the same answer. There and then, full of the Holy Spirit, I commanded him to go on his knees. We prayed in the name of Jesus and cast the demons out of the boy. While they were coming out, they twisted this boy's body like a tire of a car. Then suddenly, he fainted. When he awoke later, he was free in Jesus' name.

We could not have cast out those demons with our own authority, but because we receive the infilling of the Holy Spirit, we are empowered to do what Jesus Christ did when He was on earth. For He said in John 14:12-13:

*"I tell you the truth, anyone who has faith in Me will do what I have been doing. He will do even greater things than these, because I am going to the Father. And I will do whatever you ask in my name, so that the Son may bring glory to the Father."*

With what we did in the name of Jesus, we were fulfilling what He has commanded us to do in this world. It brings glory and honor to His name. We could not have done it without the Holy Spirit empowering us to remain steadfast in Christ Jesus.

It is the Holy Spirit that helps us grow in our faith in the Lord. So stay blessed with the anointing of the Lord the Holy Spirit.

# CHAPTER 3

# ABILITY TO HEAR FROM GOD

Every man is created in the image and likeness of God and has the capacity and the ability to hear from God, just as Abraham heard from God.

In the beginning of creation, one of the gifts God gave man was communication; that is the ability to hear and understand when God speaks and the ability to speak back to God.

In Genesis 1:28-30, it is recorded that when God made man in His own image and likeness, He said these words to man:

*28. God blessed them and said to them, "Be fruitful and increase in number, fill the earth and*

*subdue it. Rule over the fish of the sea and the birds of the air and over every living creature that moves on the ground."*
29. *Then God said, "I give you every seed bearing plant on the face of the whole earth and every tree that has fruit with seed in it. They will be yours for food.*
30. *And to all the beasts of the earth and all the birds of the air and all the creatures that move on the ground, everything that has the breath of life in it I give every green plant for food." And it was so.*

With the above scriptures it is very clear that the man God made in His own image and likeness was able hear clearly, God's instructions, or let us say, man was able to understand God's guidelines when they were given and man knew what to do. According to these scriptures, God communicated with man until man went against God's instruction and disobeyed Him. It was after man (both Adam and Eve) disobeyed God that the blaming game started. Man hid from God and later lost that intimate relationship with God, mans' Creator. After that it became very clear that man became more attached to the things of this world, instead of God, and finally lost touch with God.

Despite mans' disobedience and sin, God still spoke over and over again, but man would not listen, nor care to know if God still speaks or not. Although sins of men have become a barrier between man and God, He still finds a way to communicate with man.

From the time of the fall of Adam and Eve until Jesus came on earth, God was still speaking to His creation - sometimes through His chosen prophets, at other times, through anyone He chose as fit to use.

## THE WORK OF JESUS CHRIST

We Christians think Jesus Christ only came to take away the sins of the world. He came to do more for mankind than we will ever imagine, even though the book of Isaiah 53 tells us much of what He came to do for us.

We know Jesus Christ took up our infirmities and carried our sorrows. He was pierced for our transgressions. He was crushed for our iniquities; the punishment that brought us peace was upon Him, and by His wounds we are healed. He bore the sin of many, and made intercession for the transgressors. It is not only all of this that Jesus had done for mankind; He rebuilt or mended the broken relationship between mankind and the Father. It is not only our broken relationship that He mended but He rebuilt our right to communication with our heavenly Father, so that anytime we go to the Father in the name of Jesus, He hears us and communicates back to us through the Holy Spirit, that He has poured out on earth, for those who humble themselves to receive Him.

Jesus said these words in John 16:13-15:

*13."But when He, the Spirit of truth comes, He will not speak on His own, He will speak only*

*what He hears, and He will tell you what is yet to come.*
14. *He will bring glory to Me by taking from what is mine and making it known to you.*
15. *All that belongs to the Father is mine. That is why I said the Spirit will take from what is mine and make it known to you."*

From the scriptures above, we see the Trinity (God the Father, God the Son, and God the Holy Spirit) again at work, the coordination between the Father, the Son, and the Holy Spirit. No divine Person does anything without the other, they work in unity. That is why Jesus said that all that belongs to the Father is Jesus' as well. This proves or confirms what John said in the book of John 1 which reads: *"In the beginning was the Word, and the Word was with God, and the Word was God. He was with God in the beginning. Through Him all things were made; without Him nothing was made that has been made. In Him was life, and that life was the light of man."*

Jesus is that Word. He was there with God from the beginning. That is why Jesus made the statement, *"All that belongs to the Father is mine."* I will say it again. Jesus is the Word, and the Word is the sword of the Spirit.

Do you remember the vision that Apostle John saw on the island of Patmos in the book of Revelation? It reads: *"In His right hand He held seven stars, and out of His mouth came a sharp double edged sword. His face was like the sun shining in all its brilliance."*

Jesus' name is that double edged sword, with which, in His name, we who believe, can lead a sinner to receive salvation, and at the same time set free those who are possessed by the devil. It is in His name that we can cast out those evil spirits and set the captives free in Christ Jesus.

We need to know this truth and not treat that precious name of Jesus Christ carelessly. We need to know that the name of Jesus has power. That is why demons flee at the mention of His name.

The Bible tells us: **"Therefore God exalted Him to the highest place and gave Him the name that is above every name, that at the name of Jesus every knee should bow, in heaven and on earth and under the earth, and every tongue confess that Jesus Christ is Lord, to the glory of God the Father."**

When we come before the throne of God, we come in Jesus' name, and when the Father looks at us He does not see us as sinners, but sees us righteous in His Son Jesus. Anything that we ask in Jesus' name, He assured us He will do for us, that the Son (Jesus) may bring glory to the Father. So hold fast to this truth and never let it go.

## LISTEN TO HIS VOICE

Jesus said in the book of John 10:14-16:

*14."I am the good shepherd; I know My sheep and My sheep know Me.*

*15. Just as the Father knows Me and I know the Father and I lay down my life for the sheep.*
*16. I have other sheep that are not of this sheep pen. I must bring them also. They too will listen to My voice, and there shall be one flock and one shepherd*

If we who believe in Christ Jesus are His sheep then what He is saying to us is that when He speaks we should be able to hear or listen to His voice. That means, we who are in Christ Jesus have the ability to hear and identify His voice. He assured us again with these words in the same book of John 10:3-5:

*3. The watchman opens the gate for Him, and the sheep listen to His voice. He calls His own sheep by name and leads them out.*
*4. When He has brought out all His own, He goes on ahead of them, and His sheep follow Him because they know His voice.*
*5. But they will never follow a stranger; in fact, they will run away from him because they do not recognize a stranger's voice.*

We who are in Christ Jesus should be able to identify His voice. (The voice of the Trinity is one, you hear one you hear them all.) Humanly speaking it is very difficult to identify someone's voice if you do not spend time with that someone. It will be difficult to know His voice, if one does not spend time with Jesus in prayer and reading of His word and waiting on Him. As we have read before, it is the Holy Spirit that Jesus Christ said will reveal to us what He, Jesus has spoken. So for us to be able to hear and identify the voice of the Holy Spirit we need to pray always in the Holy Spirit.

Some may say because they are not a pastor, Evangelist, a prophet or a priest they are unable to hear from God. If you are thinking that way you need to repent. For the Bible tells us in 1 Peter 2:9 who we are in Christ Jesus.

***"But you are a chosen people, a royal priesthood, a holy nation, a people belonging to God, that you may declare the praises of Him who called you out of darkness into His wonderful light."***

We who are saved are part of that category of priest or prophet to hear from God because of the finished work of Christ Jesus. It is because of Jesus we are that chosen people of God and we should take pride in Christ Jesus, exalt His Holy name now and forever more.

I remember when I first received the infilling of the Holy Spirit, no one told me to continue to pray in the Holy Spirit. But I was so excited about my new tongue or call it my new prayer language that to this day, I always wake up very early every morning to pray in it. As time went by I started hearing the Holy Spirit speak to me. As soon as I knew it was my God who was speaking to me, I started writing the messages down. It was amazing to know all that I came to know, in Christ Jesus.

I will share with you one of messages that I had

trouble with when I used my human senses, but later on it was proven correct. When I was praying one morning as I do, the Lord told me about a woman in our group. The Lord said she had been responding to the call for healing. He said I should let her know that the Lord says she could not receive her healing unless she forgave her husband.

As soon as I heard those words, I could no longer pray, because, in my own eyes, I could not imagine this woman bearing a grudge against anyone. Secondly, I did not know how I could stand before her to deliver that kind of message. I wondered for days, but the Lord had mercy on me and made it very easy for me. I was in the church hall a few days after, and she walked up to me and said, "Elijah, I know you have a message for me." (Around this group of Christians everyone knows and calls me Elijah.) That was the first time she ever came to ask for a message of the Lord from me, and I said, "Yes! I do have one for you." I told her what the Lord had told me about her not receiving her healing. To my relief, she told me it is true, she had a grudge against her husband. She then told the whole story of what had happened. I saw her point of view for not forgiving her husband, but the Almighty God had seen that it was setting her back from receiving her healing, and the Lord wanted her to repent of her unforgiving heart so that she could be healed.

An unforgiving heart is always a hindrance to receiving the gift of healing, the healing that Jesus has already won for us, by the stripes that He received in

His body for us. So the two of us talked about it and she promised to go to her husband once and for all to talk about it and then she would forgive him as the Lord had requested.

This showed to me the depth that the Holy Spirit is willing to go in order to help all who believe in Christ Jesus receive their blessings from their Father, the Almighty God.

## DO NOT LIMIT GOD

Do not in any way limit the Almighty God in what He can do. God will always be God. Remember He has no equal. He is God by Himself. There is nothing impossible for Him. Nobody should limit God in the way He communicates with His children on earth. We may know one way but He speaks to others in total different ways, and we have to respect that instead of trying to prove that He speaks only one way and one way only. If that is the way we think, then we do not really know who God is.

Since the time of creation, God has been communicating or speaking to man whom He made in His image and likeness.

Here are some of the ways that we have seen in the Bible. He speaks face to face with man. We know He spoke face to face with Adam and Eve, Moses, and Abraham and others. He even spoke through a donkey to Balaam, the seer, in the book of Numbers, chapter 22.

He speaks through visions, dreams and prophesies. The Bible tells us in the book of Joel these will happen in the last days. Sometimes we take dreams for granted but in Job 33:14-18, the Word of God says:

*14. For God does speak now one way, now another though man may not perceive it.*
*15. In a dream, in a vision of the night, when deep sleep falls on man as they slumber in their beds,*
*16. He may speak in their ears and terrify them with warnings.*
*17. To turn man from wrongdoing and keep him from pride,*
*18. To preserve his soul from the pit, his life from perishing by the sword.*

The scriptures have confirmed that dreams are one of the ways God reaches out to His children. If you know God speaks to you in dreams, it will be right if you write down your dreams. As God has given you the dreams, He will give you also the ability to understand and interpret them. If God speaks to anyone through the gift of visions, that person has also the ability to understand the visions God will show. If not, that person should pray for that ability. We should understand the truth that God will not give a child of His a boat without a paddle. He will not give you a gift of visions without the ability to understand or interpret them.

God speaks through His angels to man. God

speaks through people we may consider as enemies, because there are some things that we may be doing wrong but nobody has the courage to tell us we are wrong. So He will use an enemy to tell us. We have to open our ears and our hearts to negative things said about us, even if we are hurt by them, may be we need to change. We do not need to be defensive about everything bad being said about us. There may be truth in what is being said and to know it is to have opportunity to repent and change our ways. If not we will be heading for a fall.

God has spoken through children and will continue to do so until the end of time. We know He spoke through Samuel to Eli the priest, when Samuel was just a young boy.

He speaks in many other ways to His children that we even do not know a thing about. Until it is revealed to us, let us hold onto all His promises.

I am not a Pastor. I am not a minister, nor do I hold any position in a Church. I am simply a child of God, but I can tell you that God has spoken to me in so many different ways. Each time, no matter in what way He chooses, I know He is the one speaking to me.

Sometimes He speaks in my spirit and I know His voice. Sometimes it is like a tape recorder opened within my spirit and I have to find a paper and a pen to write as fast as I can, all that He is telling me.

He speaks to me through the pages of the Bible. He speaks to me through songs, through preaching or teaching of His word. Most of all He speaks to me loud and clear, like a friend standing right next to me.

I remember I was about nineteen years old, a Roman Catholic boy, when I first heard God speak loudly and clearly to me. I will try to make this long story short. I am a Ghanaian by birth. It was during late 1966-67 that the Germans came to establish a vocational training school in Ghana. Because the classrooms were not ready and they were going to use a temporary building for a classroom, they wanted a limited number of trainees. The qualification of trainees needed, was to have completed two to five years of technical schooling. When I saw this opportunity in the newspaper, I applied, even though I did not complete my second year in technical school because of financial difficulty. Despite that, I was invited to take the examination. Knowing I could not qualify on my own, I went to God in prayer. On the day of the exam I realized that there were thousands who had already taken the exams, and the number of trainees needed was only sixteen.

Prayerfully I took the exam, believing in my God that I would make it even though I was up against others whom I knew had completed their education and even had a diploma. After the exam I waited prayerfully for the results. Finally they came, announcing that I was successful in the exam that I took and I was invited to be one of the sixteen who were to start the three years of training. When I received this good news, I went to God and I thanked Him for the great thing He had done for me, for one thing I knew was that I did not pass this exam because I am smart. No, I am not, and it was God who opened that door of opportunity for me.

The day to report to the centre came, and I went. When I saw the other fifteen I became so frightened. They all looked bigger than me, they had all completed their education to the extent that they had a certificate or a diploma, and moreover, they were all well dressed. I was the only one wearing shorts with my only tennis shoes. With this in mind you can imagine how frightened I was. I remember my fears drove me into a corner, but it was right there and then that my God showed up. He spoke to me very loudly and very clearly. He said; **"Do not be afraid. Know this - the teacher will not give you an examination on subjects he has not yet taught. All you have to do is to study what you are taught."**

With these words from my God it was as if I was filled with new strength to face them all.

Before the beginning of the three years of training, we were told that at the end of the three years, the best four of the sixteen would be given scholarships to go to Germany to be trained to become instructors in the school.

Throughout the three years of training we were given examinations and I can tell you that after every exam, I always ranked somewhere between tenth and sixteenth. But I never forgot what God had told me and I held onto Him in prayer. We were being trained to become auto mechanics but we also had to be trained in additional trades such as auto body building, blacksmithing, auto electrical, welding and beach fitting.

One day during the second year of our training, I was called to the office of the acting director, who was also my instructor in the auto body section. He asked me if I would want to change my vocation to auto body mechanic. I told him that I will not, but he assured me that if I would change my vocation, I would receive a scholarship there and then. I asked him to give me some time to think about it and I would come back to him with an answer. In the end, I accepted the scholarship. In the office of the director, during my second year, I signed the papers for my scholarship. This was brought to the attention of the whole class. As a result, I was hated and had other trainees come to me face to face and say, "We are going to prove to you and all the Germans, during the final exam, that they have given the scholarship to the wrong trainee." When I heard all these words, I went to God for comfort.

At the final exam, all I depended on was my God for help and He showed up again in a big way. I will say again that I was not the smartest in that class of sixteen but with God who is my strength, I was able to outrank every other trainee. I was the best of them all. My God silenced each and every one of them. When God is with you, anyone who comes against you will always fail.

Never limit what God can do for you. Remember He is the creator of heaven and earth. There is nothing impossible for Him. All we need to do is to put our trust in Him.

In everything, seek the counsel of the Lord in prayer. Whatever He tells you, hold fast onto His word, for His word fails not.

## HINDRANCES TO HEARING

The problem we face as Christians is that not many of us know the fact that every child of God has the ability to hear from God, our heavenly Father. Many leading churches today do not know this truth and so are not able to relay it to the saints that they lead. As this truth is not known or taught, whenever these saints hear it somewhere else, they harden their hearts not to believe this simple truth of God.

So unbelief sometimes comes because saints have not heard their leaders talk about these subjects, in order for them to know who they are in Christ and to receive all the promises of the Father. For that reason they are held back in their unbelief, which is the number one hindrance to hear from God.

Too much gossip can be a hindrance to hearing from God. You know that God sometimes wants to keep some things secret from others, so if you are a person who runs your mouth like a motor, speaking everything you hear, God will hold back things from you and you may end up not hearing at all from Him.

An unforgiving spirit will prevent you from hearing from God. An unforgiving heart is against God's command which says, **"If you hold anything against anyone forgive him, so that your Father in**

**heaven may forgive you your sins."** Anyone harboring an unforgiving spirit is disobedient to God, and that person will not be hearing from God. A message for him or her is to repent.

Another person who will not be hearing from God is the one God has spoken to so many times, but will not do what God has said. God will not keep on talking forever about the same thing. He will eventually stop talking, for it is said, 'a word to a wise is enough.' In the first book of Samuel, chapters two and three bear testimony of this truth. Eli, the priest of Israel at that time knew how wicked and sinful his two sons were before God. Yet he did not remove them from their place of worship before the Lord. Even though God sent a prophet to Eli about his two sons, he did not do a thing about them. Therefore, as it is recorded, *"In those days the word of the Lord was rare; there were not many visions."*

All of this is not written to make anyone afraid, but to build you up with the truth so that you may be able to enjoy fully everything that our heavenly Father has blessed us with in Christ Jesus.

In Second Peter 1:3, it reads, *"His divine power has given us everything we need for life and godliness through our knowledge of Him who called us by His own glory and goodness."*

We must be diligent in study to know our God fully and put into practice everything we know from the scriptures. By doing so, we can take pride to say we know and understand the Lord our God.

If you hear God speak and you do not understand

fully what He means, please do not lean onto your own understanding, but go to Him in prayer, and the Helper, the Holy Spirit will make things clearer to you. That is the love of God, that He wants all of His children to know the truth. It is the truth that will set us free.

I will tell you something that happened to me. I always wake up very early, every morning, to praise and worship my Lord and then go back to sleep for a few hours before going to work. This particular day, I woke up about an hour or so earlier to pray and then went back to sleep. I overslept. When I opened my eyes and looked at the clock, I jumped from the bed. As soon as my foot touched the floor I heard the Lord said to me loudly and clearly, *"Remain in My love."*

At the time that He spoke these words to me I was totally in my flesh, because all that I was thinking of at that moment was work, causing me to misunderstand what God had said. I began questioning God, asking what did I do wrong that I am not in your love and you are asking me to remain in your love?

I became worried, and I went back in my mind over everything that I had said or done weeks before, but could not pinpoint anything that I could say had derailed me from the love of God. It took me a week to understand what God had said.

I was driving to work, listening to Bible reading, when all of sudden a preacher came on the radio, reading from John 15:9, where it reads, *"As the Father has loved Me, so have I loved you. Now remain in My love."*

As soon as I heard these words, He started to explain to me what He had meant, when He told me to remain in His love. He explained that if I were not already in His love, He would not have told me to remain there. It is because I am already there in His love, that is the reason He was telling me to remain in His love.

Praise God for His unfailing love. I always understand my Lord when I am led by the Spirit and not leaning onto my own understanding. So let us all watch out as far as God's word is concerned not to lean on our own understanding, for if we do we will surely miss what He is really saying to us as His children whom He loves.

Remember this always. God Almighty loves you so much, more than you will ever know or imagine. He is doing everything to reach you. All you need to do is to open up your heart to Him and obey Him. He will lead you by His Spirit to enter into all the blessings that He has for you before the beginning of the world. If only we are willing and obedient He said, we who are called by His name, will surely eat the good of the land.

There is something we all have to be mindful of, the ones who hear from God. We have to know that sometimes our strong will gets in the way of God. It should not be that way. Sometimes we desire something so much that we even go to the extent to say, "I HEARD IT FROM GOD." We can not force our strong will on God, nor can we twist His mighty hands to accept our evil will.

Let us get this very clear. If God has not spoken to you and you go before anybody to say God said to me this and that, remember, you are lying in God's name and you need to stop and repent. Remember always that He is the Creator of heaven and earth. He holds the whole world in His mighty hands. He can destroy you in a second. You need to fear Him, not to lie in His name.

If you have a strong desire for something and have already made up your mind about whatever that thing may be, do not waste God's time trying to ask Him to agree to your wishes. Treat the Creator as one who knows everything and He is the only one who can give the best or show you the best. Whenever we go to God the Father in Jesus' name, let us learn to empty ourselves out, ask for His counseling, His direction and His guidelines. Whenever we do that, when He speaks and directs us we will never go wrong.

## FINAL WORDS

Finally, to all my brothers and sisters in Christ Jesus we have to bear in mind that we are a very blessed generation. We have God the Father, who loves us so much to send us salvation through His Son Christ Jesus and we know through Him we have our redemption. By His grace we have the out pouring of the Holy Spirit on earth, and all we need to do is to humble ourselves before Him and He will lead us into all His truth. In that way, we will not follow every teaching but the truth according to His word. God said in His word in Jeremiah 9:23-24:

**23. This is what the Lord says: *"Let not the wise man boast of his wisdom or the strong man boast of his strength or the rich man boast of his riches.***
**24. But let him who boasts boast about this: <u>that he understands and knows Me, that I AM the Lord who exercises kindness, justice and righteousness on earth, for in this I delight.</u>"**

With this truth let us seek the Lord diligently with all our hearts, day and night. Let us spend time to study His word and get to know Him, and the Holy Spirit will help us to understand everything we need to know about our God so that we can play our part in His new revival on earth.

This is my prayer for all the saints of the Lord:

Heavenly Father, in the name of Jesus Christ, I commit all your children who are called by your name into your mighty hand. Touch our hearts and renew our hearts. Fill our hearts with your true love so that we can love you the way we are to love you. Teach us to love your ways and to love one another.

Renew our minds so that we can understand your truth, and be the doers of your word, for your word is the truth. Help us by the mighty power of the Holy Spirit to understand the depth of your sacrificial death on the cross for our sins and the power of your resurrection. Help us to be bold and true witnesses of your unfailing love.

Thank you Father, for hearing our heart cry and answering all our prayers, in Jesus' mighty name we pray.

Amen and Amen.

# PRAYER OF SALVATION

If you do not know **Jesus** as your **Savior and Lord** simply pray the following prayer in faith and the **Lord Jesus** will be your **Lord.**

Heavenly Father I come to You in the name of **Jesus.** Your Word says, "Whosoever shall call on the name of the **Lord Jesus** shall be saved." and "If thou shall confess with thy mouth the **Lord Jesus**, and shall believe in your heart that God raised Him from the dead, you shall be saved. (Acts 2:2; Romans 10:9)

**Lord**, I take You at Your **Word.** I confess that **Jesus** is **Lord.** I believe in my heart that You raised Him from the dead. Forgive me of all my sins and come into my heart and be the **Lord** of my life.

Thank **You Lord** for coming into my heart and saving me. Amen

If you have prayed this prayer, I advise you to find a Bible based local church, and become a member. Learn more about **Jesus** and the power of His resurrection.

ISBN 142512749-5

Made in United States
Orlando, FL
16 December 2024